WISDOM
— *of the* —
EARTH

VISIONS OF AN ECOLOGICAL FAITH

Volume 1: Ancient Christianity

Edited and Photographed by
Gordon Miller

• Green Rock Press •
Seattle

WISDOM OF THE EARTH:
VISIONS OF AN ECOLOGICAL FAITH

First Edition

Cataloging Information
(provided by publisher)

Miller, Gordon.

WISDOM OF THE EARTH:
VISIONS OF AN ECOLOGICAL FAITH.

Vol. 1: **Ancient Christianity.**

1. Nature–Religious aspects–Christianity.
2. Nature photography.
I. Title.

ISBN 0-9647007-1-9

Library of Congress Catalog
Card Number 95-77679

✪ *This book is printed on recycled paper.*

WISDOM
of the Earth

The books in this set present the best creation-centered literature of the Judeo-Christian tradition, and enhance the meaning and beauty of the words through insightful nature photography. They promote a Christian vision that encompasses not only human life but the life of the whole creation, a vision with both spiritual promise and ethical responsibilities.

The guiding theme of the books is the notion of Wisdom. In the Wisdom literature of ancient Israel, Wisdom is the principle, or personification, of cosmic order and intelligence. The ways of Wisdom are the supreme object of inquiry, and thinking and acting in harmony with these ways is the highest human calling. Wisdom in this sense bears a similarity to the *Dharma* and the *Tao* in other religions. Early in the Christian era, Wisdom became identified with Christ, the *Logos*, signifying the deep love of the Creator for the creation. Wisdom in its various forms has thus shaped Christian thinking through the centuries, and continues to provide a way to integrate Heaven and Earth—the cosmic and the historical, the spiritual and the material dimensions of the Christian faith.

Volume 1 of the set is devoted to ancient Christianity, and includes selections from the Bible and the Fathers of the Church up through the eighth century. Volume 2 will cover medieval and modern Christianity, with passages from Celtic writers, Hildegard of Bingen, St. Francis, and many other authors from the Renaissance and Reformation up through the twentieth century.

*D*oes not wisdom call,
and does not understanding raise her voice?
On the heights, beside the way, at the crossroads,
she takes her stand; beside the gates in front of the town,
at the entrance of the portals she cries out:
"To you, O people, I call, and my cry is to all that live.
O simple ones, learn prudence;
acquire intelligence, you who lack it.

The Lord created me at the beginning of his work,
the first of his acts of long ago.
Ages ago I was set up, at the first,
before the beginning of the earth.
When there were no depths I was brought forth,
when there were no springs abounding with water.
Before the mountains had been shaped,
before the hills, I was brought forth—
when he had not yet made earth and fields,
or the world's first bits of soil.
When he established the heavens, I was there,
when he drew a circle on the face of the deep,
when he made firm the skies above,
when he established the fountains of the deep,
when he assigned to the sea its limit,
so that the waters might not transgress his command,
when he marked out the foundations of the earth,
then I was beside him, like a master worker;
and I was daily his delight, rejoicing before him always,
rejoicing in his inhabited world
and delighting in the human race."

Proverbs 8:1-5, 22-31

CONTENTS

ACKNOWLEDGEMENTS

My sincere thanks to the people who have supported this book through its fledgling stages and have helped it to fly. First and foremost, my wife, Jacquelyn, lent an attentive ear and a helpful mind and hand, displayed great patience during my photographic pursuits, and contributed encouragement without ceasing. My parents eagerly assisted me in locating and photographing various natural things, particularly bird's nests and butterflies. Jo Gershman was an imaginative artistic advisor, while Danny Burnstein was a most apt and agreeable photographic subject. Tim Dillon offered welcome advice on the text, along with sympathetic inspiration. Burrell Dickey created an elegant design for the book to complement the inherent beauty of its message. And Rocky Rhodes of Green Rock Press provided the multifaceted support of a publisher and the fellowship of a friend in the process of transforming the words and images into the finished book.

INTRODUCTION

One of the deep fascinations of my teenage years centered around the phenomenon of frog eggs. I would search them out in the springtime forests of southern Indiana, feeling the pulse of the season in my eager heart. Even though the humble ponds and puddles where I usually found the eggs could evoke no images of the primordial deep, they nevertheless held, in those translucent jellylike blobs punctuated by particles of black, an intimation of the mystery of life. I would observe the eggs daily, and during the following weeks, and repeatedly over the years, would contemplate the sublime process through which the seemingly homogeneous central spheres sprouted tails and legs and gradually flourished into frogs.

When I later learned of the intricacies of genes and chromosomes, I discovered that the mystery went even deeper. For I found out that not only does the DNA provide for the dominant bodily forms that we see in any particular frog, it also offers other, unrealized or recessive possibilities as well. The simple but directed dynamism of the egg had always enthralled me; now the discovery that there was another dimension of possibility lying unsuspected within those apparently simple spheres fueled my fascination with the protean creativity at the source of life.

It is with a similar sense of reverent recognition of a surprising energy and richness in the source that many spiritual seekers have recently been discovering the wisdom in ancient religious writings. In the case of the unsuspected ecological riches of the Christian tradition, this discovery, at least for most believers, is just beginning. With eyes newly sensitized to the life and limitations of our earthly abode, readers of these venerable texts–from the Bible to a host of later works–are gaining insight into the ecological dimension of their Christian heritage. But why has this important religious element remained so long a merely recessive aspect of the faith?

In the genealogy of Christian thought in the Western world, the dominant strain of thinking has masked some important underlying possibilities. An almost exclusive emphasis on the historical Jesus has hindered an appreciation of the cosmic Christ. At the same time, concern with the powerful transcendence of God has perhaps prevented an awareness of God's sustaining immanence in all things. And a somewhat narrow focus on *human* life and history—a focus that has revealed itself most problematically in the emphasis on the domination of nature, especially in association with modern science and technology—has blurred an awareness of, and sense of responsibility for, other forms of life and the encompassing history of the whole creation. These often-overlooked themes are evident in abundance in the Bible and they infuse the writings of many Fathers of the Church.

Christian thinking about nature has thus always been a hybrid, even if its inherent multiplicity has not always been evident in its familiar outward forms. In the present climate of environmental concern, however, the long-hidden ecological elements of Christian theology are finding fuller expression. The integration of these aspects of our history into our current body of beliefs will enlarge our compassion and enrich our vision for the coming season of Christian life and thought, a transformation that will offer both environmental and spiritual benefits.

The cultivation of an ecological Christianity will involve, of course, thinking and acting in earth-friendly ways to heal and sustain the environment. Numerous local congregations and national religious organizations, motivated by the Biblical conviction that "the earth is the Lord's" and we are its stewards, have begun recycling, conserving energy, planting trees, advocating environmental justice, and preaching and teaching on ecological themes.

Active caring for creation, however, is not the only implication of these ancient ecological ideas. For the biblical writers and the Church Fathers, the inclusion of creation in their sphere of concern wasn't motivated by environmental crises; it was a natural aspect of their religious vision. We carry forward this vision when the ecological perspective, in addition to encouraging new ways of thinking and acting, also strengthens the more contemplative realm of Christian spirituality—when it engenders a new stillness in the soul. When we know, not only in our brains but in our bones, that the same creative energy that forms the tadpole into the frog also flows in our veins and brings us to spiritual maturity, we will more likely learn to loosen our grip at the helm of our hearts. Recognizing the Wisdom working within nature should strengthen our faith in the potential of the same Spirit within ourselves.

If we fail to pursue an ecological form of faith, it is thus not only the outer air and water and animals and trees that will suffer. The inner dimension, in both nature and ourselves, will wither as well. We are faced as a species with the challenge of overcoming anthropocentrism in our relations to the natural world. We are faced as individuals with the moment-to-moment task of overcoming egocentrism in our relations to people and things. And the two challenges are merely different aspects of the same spiritual vocation, our response to which will shape both the future of the earth and the metamorphosis of the spirit.

In the pages that follow, a variety of ancient voices bear witness to the significance of creation in the Judeo-Christian tradition. Part One draws out some of the most important ecological themes of the Old and New Testaments. The passages contain both rather literal references to the natural world, as well as more metaphorical uses of natural phenomena to convey spiritual truths, such as in the parables of Jesus. There is divine magic in these metaphors. We typically tend to see a mustard seed, a grain of wheat, or a rush of wind as a merely material thing which, in parables, can be used to illustrate things belonging to an essentially distinct non-material realm.

But such metaphors could be understood further as an effort to unify these two worlds, to tie the dominion of God in nature to the kingdom of God in the soul, thus doing justice to both the cosmic and the human dimensions of the Incarnation. Those who have ears to hear, then, are able to discern the divine Word in the world because they have heard the Voice within. Part of the challenge of an ecological Christianity is to see if, in some way, the objects of nature can once again become living symbols of spiritual realities.

Part Two contains selections from the voluminous writings of the Church Fathers, both Eastern and Western, spanning the second through the eighth centuries. Many more passages could have been included, of course, but space would not allow. The voices of the Fathers are not always in simple unison, but instead form more of a collective conversation, or, in their more lyrical moments, a chorus of several parts. All of the Fathers were deeply immersed in the Scriptures, and their writings form an important ancient lens through which modern Christians can gain a somewhat different, and perhaps deeper, perspective on Biblical themes.

But they were also insightful interpreters of the Word of God in nature, and they invite their readers to learn this divine language written, or spoken, in the water and the wind, in the living and dying of animals, and in the passing of the seasons. The Biblical promise of "a new heaven and a new earth" informed their vision, and they looked forward with hope to the time when every atom would declare, and every ear would hear, the divine Word resonating throughout the height and depth of the cosmos.

The photographs, like the passages, also range from the more literal to the metaphorical or symbolic. They are meant to highlight and to amplify the Voice of the earth, in accord with its expression in the accompanying texts, and to provide perhaps an intimation of the new creation. I hope that they will turn you toward the earth itself, with an observant eye and a listening heart.

Part One

BIBLICAL ROOTS

The Old Testament

A fundamental theme of the Hebrew Scriptures of ancient Israel is the goodness of the earth. This conviction surfaces repeatedly in the Genesis refrain that "God saw that it was good" and it bursts forth in abundance in the Psalms, with the goodness of the earth inevitably seen as an aspect of the overflowing goodness of God. On the broad cultural and religious stage shaped by this conviction there occurred what is perhaps the central drama of biblical faith–God's gift of good land. The God who led the people of Israel out of bondage in Egypt into the responsible freedom and fullness of the promised land was not only the Lord of human history, but also, and above all, "the Lord of heaven and earth," the creator and sustainer of the earth and all its inhabitants, both humans and animals. The "dust of the ground," called in Hebrew *adamah*, gave humankind not only its bodily substance but also its name. And the land of Israel, which was permeated by the soul of its people, gave to the Israelites not only their sustenance but also their sense of identity. This "creation faith" of the Israelites eventually extended itself, especially in the prophets, into the expectation of a universal re-creation, the promise of "new heavens and a new earth."

Throughout the entire story of the Old Testament, from creation to the hoped-for new creation, God works in the world through the divine Word and Wisdom. The Word called all things into existence in the beginning; Wisdom "pervades and penetrates" the entire creation and "renews all things." Through cosmic Wisdom the goodness of God becomes manifest in the earth, and through this Wisdom working in the hearts and minds of humankind the descendants of Adam become grounded in God and find their proper habitation in the good land.

In the beginning when God created the heavens and the earth, the earth was a formless void and darkness covered the face of the deep, while a wind from God swept over the face of the waters. Then God said, "Let there be light"; and there was light. And God saw that the light was good; and God separated the light from the darkness. God called the light Day, and the darkness he called Night. And there was evening and there was morning, the first day.

Genesis 1:1-5

T he heavens are
telling the glory of God; and the firmament
proclaims his handiwork. Day to day pours forth
speech, and night to night declares knowledge.
There is no speech, nor are there words;
their voice is not heard; yet their voice goes out
through all the earth, and their words to the end
of the world.

Psalm 19:1-4

The voice of the Lord is over the waters;
the God of glory thunders, the Lord, over
mighty waters. The voice of the Lord is
powerful; the voice of the Lord is full of majesty.

The voice of the Lord flashes forth flames
of fire. The voice of the Lord shakes the
wilderness…

Psalm 29:3-4, 7-8

The earth is the Lord's and all that is in it, the world, and those who live in it; for he has founded it on the seas, and established it on the rivers.

Who shall ascend the hill of the Lord? And who shall stand in his holy place? Those who have clean hands and pure hearts, who do not lift up their souls to what is false, and do not swear deceitfully. They will receive blessing from the Lord, and vindication from the God of their salvation.

Psalm 24:1-5

he Lord your God
is bringing you into a good land, a land with
flowing streams, with springs and underground
waters welling up in valleys and hills, a land of
wheat and barley, of vines and fig trees and
pomegranates, a land of olive trees and honey,
a land where you may eat bread without scarcity,
where you will lack nothing, a land whose
stones are iron and from whose hills you may
mine copper. You shall eat your fill and bless
the Lord your God for the good land that he
has given you.

Deuteronomy 8:7-10

*Y*ou shall observe my statutes and faithfully keep my ordinances, so that you may live on the land securely. The land will yield its fruit, and you will eat your fill and live on it securely… The land shall not be sold in perpetuity, for the land is mine; with me you are but aliens and tenants."

Leviticus 25:18-19, 23

"Keep, then, this entire commandment that I am commanding you today, so that you may have strength to go in and occupy the land that you are crossing over to occupy, and so that you may live long in the land that the Lord swore to your ancestors to give them and to their descendants, a land flowing with milk and honey. For the land that you are about to enter to occupy is not like the land of Egypt, from which you have come, where you sow your seed and irrigate by foot like a vegetable garden. But the land that you are crossing over to occupy is a land of hills and valleys, watered by rain from the sky, a land that the Lord your God looks after. The eyes of the Lord your God are always on it, from the beginning of the year to the end of the year."

Deuteronomy 11:8-12

ut where
shall wisdom be found?

God understands the way to it, and he knows
its place. For he looks to the ends of the earth,
and sees everything under the heavens.
When he gave to the wind its weight,
and apportioned out the waters by measure;
when he made a decree for the rain,
and a way for the thunderbolt;
then he saw it and declared it;
he established it, and searched it out.
And he said to humankind,
"Truly, the fear of the Lord, that is wisdom;
and to depart from evil is understanding."

Job 28:12, 23-28

*A*sk the animals,
and they will teach you; the birds of the air, and
they will tell you; ask the plants of the earth, and
they will teach you; and the fish of the sea will
declare to you. Who among all these does not
know that the hand of the Lord has done this?
In his hand is the life of every living thing
and the breath of every human being.

Job 12:7-10

For the fate of humans and the fate of animals is
the same; as one dies, so dies the other. They all
have the same breath, and humans have no
advantage over the animals; for all is vanity.
All go to one place; all are from the dust, and all
turn to dust again.

Ecclesiastes 3:19-20

Your steadfast love, O Lord, extends to
the heavens, your faithfulness to the clouds.
Your righteousness is like the mighty mountains,
your judgements are like the great deep;
you save humans and animals alike, O Lord.

Psalm 36:5-9

O Lord my God, you are very great.
You are clothed with honor and majesty, wrapped in
light as with a garment. You stretch out the heavens like
a tent, you set the beams of your chambers on the
waters, you make the clouds your chariot,
you ride on the wings of the wind, you make the winds
your messengers, fire and flame your ministers.

You make springs gush forth in the valleys; they flow
between the hills, giving drink to every wild animal; the
wild asses quench their thirst. By the streams the birds
of the air have their habitation; they sing among the
branches. From your lofty abode you water the mountains; the earth is satisfied with the fruit of
your work.

You cause the grass to grow for the cattle, and plants for
people to use, to bring forth food from the earth,
and wine to gladden the human heart, oil to make the
face shine, and bread to strengthen the human heart.

O Lord, how manifold are your works! In wisdom you
have made them all; the earth is full of your creatures.
Yonder is the sea, great and wide, creeping things innumerable are there, living things both small and great.

May the glory of the Lord endure forever…

Psalm 104:1-4, 10-15, 24-25, 31

Wisdom, the fashioner of all things, taught me. There is in her a spirit that is intelligent, holy… For wisdom is more mobile than any motion; because of her pureness she pervades and penetrates all things. For she is a breath of the power of God, and a pure emanation of the glory of the Almighty; therefore nothing defiled gains entrance into her. For she is a reflection of eternal light, a spotless mirror of the working of God, and an image of his goodness. Although she is but one, she can do all things, and while remaining in herself, she renews all things; in every generation she passes into holy souls and makes them friends of God.

Wisdom of Solomon 7:22, 24-27

*D*o not remember the former things, or consider the things of old. I am about to do a new thing; now it springs forth, do you not perceive it? I will make a way in the wilderness and rivers in the desert. The wild animals will honor me, the jackals and the ostriches; for I give water in the wilderness, rivers in the desert.

Isaiah 43:18-20

The wolf shall live with the lamb, the leopard shall lie down with the kid, the calf and the lion and the fatling together, and a little child shall lead them. The cow and the bear shall graze, their young shall lie down together; and the lion shall eat straw like the ox. The nursing child shall play over the hole of the asp, and the weaned child shall put its hand on the adder's den. They will not hurt or destroy on all my holy mountain; for the earth will be full of the knowledge of the Lord as the waters cover the sea.

Isaiah 11:6-9

or I am about to create new heavens and a new earth; the former things shall not be remembered or come to mind. But be glad and rejoice forever in what I am creating.

Isaiah 65:17-18

The New Testament

The creative Word and Wisdom of God that formed and fed the land of Israel and transformed its people, became, in the New Testament, the Word made flesh. The figure of the historical Jesus, who was born in a manger and brought wholeness to the sick and sinful, was at the same time the cosmic Christ, "the firstborn of all creation" in whom "all things hold together." His vision and purpose, and that of his early followers, thus encompassed both the redemption of human beings and the salvation of the entire creation, both the life of the church and the renovation of the cosmos. His teaching concerning the Kingdom of God was therefore two-dimensional: the personal and present reformation occasioned by an individual's surrendering to divine dominion in the human heart was given greater meaning and direction by being part of the universal movement of creation toward its final consummation, in which God's beneficent reign would be "all in all." In the parables of growth—of a mustard seed or a grain of wheat—the generative power of the immanent kingdom in both human life and the life of nature is particularly evident. The Apostle Paul elaborated on this theme of new life in light of the resurrection of Christ by saying that "the whole creation," including humanity, "has been groaning in labor pains," awaiting with a deep yearning the coming of "a new heaven and a new earth," a prospect glimpsed by John at the end of his Revelation. The New Testament vision of the Creator's deep involvement in this grand drama is indicated by the fact that in the familiar phrase of John 3:16--"For God so loved the world that he gave his only Son"—the Greek word used for "world" was *kosmos.*

In the beginning was the Word, and the Word was with God, and the Word was God. He was in the beginning with God. All things came into being through him, and without him not one thing came into being. What has come into being in him was life, and the life was the light of all people. The light shines in the darkness, and the darkness did not overcome it.

And the Word became flesh and lived among us, and we have seen his glory, the glory as of a father's only son, full of grace and truth.

John 1:1-5, 14

He is the image of the invisible God, the firstborn of all creation; for in him all things in heaven and on earth were created, things visible and invisible, whether thrones or dominions or rulers or powers—all things have been created through him and for him. He himself is before all things, and in him all things hold together. He is the head of the body, the church; he is the beginning, the firstborn from the dead, so that he might come to have first place in everything. For in him all the fullness of God was pleased to dwell, and through him God was pleased to reconcile to himself all things, whether on earth or in heaven, by making peace through the blood of his cross.

Colossians 1:15-20

*J*ust as the branch
cannot bear fruit by itself unless it abides in the
vine, neither can you unless you abide in me.
I am the vine, you are the branches. Those who
abide in me and I in them bear much fruit,
because apart from me you can do nothing."

John 15:4-5

o not worry
about your life, what you will eat or what you
will drink, or about your body, what you will
wear. Is not life more than food, and the body
more than clothing? Look at the birds of the
air; they neither sow nor reap nor gather into
barns, and yet your heavenly Father feeds
them. Are you not of more value than they?
And can any of you by worrying add a single
hour to your span of life? And why do you
worry about clothing? Consider the lilies of the
field, how they grow; they neither toil nor spin,
yet I tell you, even Solomon in all his glory was
not clothed like one of these."

Matthew 6:25-29

"A sower went out to sow his seed; and as he sowed, some fell on the path and was trampled on, and the birds of the air ate it up. Some fell on the rock; and as it grew up, it withered for lack of moisture. Some fell among thorns, and the thorns grew with it and choked it. Some fell into good soil, and when it grew, it produced a hundredfold."

Luke 8:5-8

"Very truly, I tell you, unless a grain of wheat falls into the earth and dies, it remains just a single grain; but if it dies, it bears much fruit. Those who love their life lose it, and those who hate their life in this world will keep it for eternal life."

John 12:24-25

He put before them another parable: "The kingdom of heaven is like a mustard seed that someone took and sowed in his field; it is the smallest of all the seeds, but when it has grown it is the greatest of shrubs and becomes a tree, so that the birds of the air come and make nests in its branches."

Matthew 13:31-32

He also said,
"The kingdom of God is as if someone would
scatter seed on the ground, and would sleep and
rise night and day, and the seed would sprout
and grow, he does not know how. The earth
produces of itself, first the stalk, then the head,
then the full grain in the head."

Mark 4:26-28

God put this power to work in Christ when he
raised him from the dead and seated him at his
right hand in the heavenly places, far above all
rule and authority and power and dominion, and
above every name that is named, not only in this
age but also in the age to come. And he has put
all things under his feet and has made him the
head over all things for the church, which is his
body, the fullness of him who fills all in all.

Ephesians 1:20-23

consider that the sufferings of this present time are not worth comparing with the glory about to be revealed to us. For the creation waits with eager longing for the revealing of the children of God; for the creation was subjected to futility, not of its own will but by the will of the one who subjected it, in hope that the creation itself will be set free from its bondage to decay and will obtain the freedom of the glory of the children of God. We know that the whole creation has been groaning in labor pains until now; and not only the creation, but we ourselves, who have the first fruits of the Spirit, groan inwardly while we wait for adoption, the redemption of our bodies.

Romans 8:18-23

hen I saw a new heaven and a
new earth; for the first heaven and the first earth had passed
away, and the sea was no more. And I saw the holy city,
the new Jerusalem, coming down out of heaven from God,
prepared as a bride adorned for her husband. And I heard a
loud voice from the throne saying,

> "See, the home of God is among mortals.
> He will dwell with them as their God;
> they will be his peoples,
> and God himself will be with them;
> he will wipe every tear from their eyes.
> Death will be no more;
> mourning and crying and pain will be no more,
> for the first things have passed away."

And the one who was seated on the throne said, "See, I am
making all things new."

Revelation 21:1-5

Part Two

CLASSICAL BRANCHES: FATHERS OF THE CHURCH

Irenaeus

Irenaeus (130?-200?) grew up in Smyrna, on the west coast of present-day Turkey, by the shores of the Aegean Sea. He was a student of Polycarp, the Greek bishop of Smyrna, who, according to tradition, had learned of the life of Christ from John, the Beloved Disciple himself. Irenaeus moved west by around 155 and in 177 became bishop of Lyons, in Gaul, where he died, perhaps as a martyr, some twenty years later. In life he was an advocate for Christian unity, and in death his writings have been an influential common source for both the Eastern and the Western theological traditions.

The primary purpose of his writings was to defend the Christian faith against the heresy of Gnosticism. In his major work, entitled *Against the Heresies*, Irenaeus opposed the Gnostic view of God as an alien, utterly transcendent deity dwelling in a realm of purely spiritual light far removed from the material darkness and evil of the earth. In place of this dualistic doctrine, Irenaeus proposed that the pinnacle of divine purpose, indeed the goal of the creation, is the transformation of matter by God's two "hands"—the Son and the Spirit, the Word and Wisdom—which brought all things into being in the beginning and even now transform them from within toward their exalted end. He therefore emphasized that "the glory of God is a living man, and the life of man consists in beholding God," a glory that was revealed and rehearsed in the Incarnation of the Word. Though Irenaeus's vision encompassed the entire creation, his focus was on the redemption and resurrection of that bit of "earth" most intimate to us—our frail flesh.

Since created things are various and numerous, they are indeed well fitted and adapted to the whole creation; yet when viewed individually, are mutually opposite and inharmonious, just as the sound of the lyre, which consists of many and opposite notes, gives rise to one unbroken melody, through means of the interval which separates each one from the others. The lover of truth therefore ought not to be deceived by the interval between each note…but should hold that one and the same person formed the whole, so as to prove the judgement, goodness, and skill exhibited in the whole work and specimen of wisdom. Those, too, who listen to the melody, ought to praise and extol the artist, to admire the tension of some notes, to attend to the softness of others, to catch the sound of others between both these extremes, …so as to inquire at what each one aims, and what is the cause of their variety.

Against the Heresies 2.25.2

ow God
shall be glorified in his handiwork, fitting it so
as to be conformable to, and modelled after,
His own Son. For by the hands of the Father,
that is, by the Son and the Holy Spirit, man,
and not merely a part of man, was made in the
likeness of God. Now the soul and the spirit
are certainly a *part* of the man, but certainly not
the man; for the perfect man consists in the
commingling and the union of the soul receiving
the spirit of the Father, and the admixture of
that fleshly nature which was moulded after the
image of God.

Against the Heresies 5.6.1

For the glory of God is a living man; and the life
of man consists in beholding God. For if the
manifestation of God which is made by means of
the creation, affords life to all living in the earth,
much more does that revelation of the Father
which comes through the Word, give life to
those who see God.

Against the Heresies 4.20.7

he Creator of the world is truly the Word of God: and this is our Lord, who in the last times was made man, existing in this world, and who in an invisible manner contains all things created, and is inherent in the entire creation, since the Word of God governs and arranges all things; and therefore He came to His own in a visible manner, and was made flesh, and hung upon a tree, that He might sum up all things in Himself.

Against the Heresies 5.18.3

*F*lesh shall also be found fit for and capable of receiving the power of God, which at the beginning received the skilful touches of God; so that one part became the eye for seeing; another, the ear for hearing; another, the hand for feeling and working; another, the sinews stretched out everywhere, and holding the limbs together; another, arteries and veins, passages for the blood and the air; another, the various internal organs; another, the blood, which is the bond of union between soul and body.

Against the Heresies 5.3.2

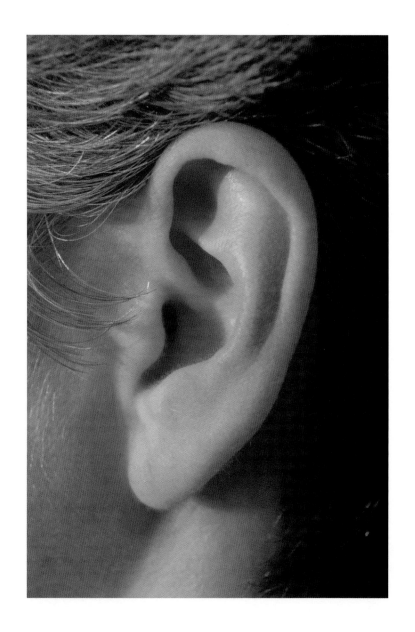

Since the Lord
has power to infuse life into what He has
fashioned, and since the flesh is capable of
being quickened, what remains to prevent its
participating in incorruption, which is a blissful
and never-ending life granted by God?

Against the Heresies 5.3.3

As a bare grain is sown, and, germinating by the
command of God its Creator, rises again,
clothed upon and glorious, but not before it has
died and suffered decomposition, and become
mingled with the earth; so it is seen from this,
that we have not entertained a vain belief in the
resurrection of the body.

Fragment 12

The predicted blessing belongs unquestionably to the times of the kingdom, when the creation, having been renovated and set free, shall fructify with an abundance of all kinds of food, from the dew of heaven, and from the fertility of the earth.

The days will come, in which vines shall grow, each having ten thousand branches, and in each branch ten thousand twigs, and in each true twig ten thousand shoots, and in each one of the shoots ten thousand clusters, and on every one of the clusters ten thousand grapes, and every grape when pressed will give five and twenty metretes of wine.

Against the Heresies 5.33.3

Neither is the substance nor the essence of the creation annihilated (for faithful and true is He who has established it), but "the *fashion* of the world passeth away;" ... But when this present fashion of things passes away, and man has been renewed, and flourishes in an incorruptible state, so as to preclude the possibility of becoming old, then there shall be the new heaven and the new earth, in which the new man shall remain continually, always holding fresh converse with God.

Against the Heresies 5.36.1

God cannot be measured in the heart, and incomprehensible is He in the mind; He who holds the earth in the hollow of His hand. Who perceives the measure of His right hand? Who knoweth His finger? Or who doth understand His hand—that hand which measures immensity; that hand which, by its own measure, spreads out the measure of the heavens, and which comprises in its hollow the earth with the abysses; which contains in itself the breadth, and length, and the deep below, and the height above of the whole creation.

Against the Heresies 4.19.2

e it is who
fills the heavens, and views the abysses, who is
also present with every one of us. For he says,
"Am I a God at hand, and not a God afar off?
If any man is hid in secret places, shall I not
see him?" For His hand lays hold of all things,
and that it is which illumines the heavens, and
lightens also the things which are under the
heavens, and trieth the reins and the hearts,
is also present in hidden things, and in our
secret thoughts, and does openly nourish and
preserve us.

Against the Heresies 4.19.2

Basil of Caesarea

Basil of Caesarea (330?-379), also known as Basil the Great, was from a family that exerted a significant formative influence on the early history of Christianity. He and his brother, Gregory of Nyssa, along with his closest friend, Gregory of Nazianzus, are the three Eastern Church Fathers known as the Cappadocians, after the region of Asia Minor, now east-central Turkey, where they were born. Basil became a dynamic teacher of rhetoric in Caesarea, but after his devout sister Macrina accused him of being puffed up with the "pride of oratory," and further shaken by the death of his brother Naucratius, he decided in 357 to follow an ascetic life. He founded a monastery by the river Iris in Annesi, again inspired in part by Macrina, who, with their mother, had already established a community of religious women, and he wrote an influential set of rules for monastic life. In 370 he became bishop of Caesarea, a post which placed him at the center of ecclesiastical politics and religious controversy. He worked tirelessly to heal divisions within the church, while at the same time assisting the poor with aid financed largely through the selling of his own inherited possessions.

Basil was of rather sturdy stock, with a sternness that perhaps reflected the ruggedness of the Cappadocian landscape, a terrain that greatly attracted his interest and admiration. His *Hexaemeron*, a series of homilies on the six days of creation recorded in Genesis, exclusive of the making of human beings, is a passionate celebration of the divine power and presence in nature, a universal presence that sets up sympathetic resonances throughout the community of creatures. Drawing both on ancient authorities and his own observations, he describes a great variety of natural phenomena, limning the lessons of this inspired language of nature, and listening for the creative Word still working in the world and bringing about what he calls "the consummation of all things."

God, before all those
things which now attract our notice existed,
after casting about in His mind and determining
to bring into being that which had no being,
imagined the world such as it ought to be,
and created matter in harmony with the form
which He wished to give it. He assigned to
the heavens the nature adapted for the heavens,
and gave to the earth an essence in accordance
with its form. He formed, as He wished, fire,
air and water, and gave to each the essence
which the object of its existence required.
Finally, He welded all the diverse parts of the
universe by links of indissoluble attachment
and established between them so perfect a
fellowship and harmony that the most distant,
in spite of their distance, appeared united in one
universal sympathy.

Hexaemeron 2.2

nd God said,
Let there be light." The first word of God
created the nature of light; it made darkness
vanish, dispelled gloom, illuminated the world,
and gave to all beings at the same time a sweet
and gracious aspect. The heavens, until then
enveloped in darkness, appeared with that beauty
which they still present to our eyes. The air was
lighted up, or rather made the light circulate
mixed with its substance, and, distributing its
splendour rapidly in every direction, so dispersed
itself to its extreme limits.

Hexaemeron 2.7

"And God said,
Let the waters under the heaven be gathered
together unto one place, and let the dry land
appear, and it was so. And God called the dry
land earth and the gathering together of the
waters called He seas."

"And God said, Let the earth bring forth grass,
the herb yielding seed, and the fruit tree yielding
fruit after his kind, whose seed is in itself."
It was deep wisdom that commanded the earth,
when it rested after discharging the weight of
the waters, first to bring forth grass, then wood,
as we see it doing still at this time. For the
voice that was then heard and this command
were as a natural and permanent law for it; it
gave fertility and the power to produce fruit for
all ages to come.

Hexaemeron 5.1

Thus nature, receiving the impulse of this first
command, follows without interruption the
course of ages, until the consummation of
all things.

Hexaemeron 5.10

"Let the earth bring forth grass;" and instantly, with useful plants, appear noxious plants; with corn, hemlock; with the other nutritious plants, hellebore, monkshood, mandrake and the juice of the poppy. What then? Shall we show no gratitude for so many beneficial gifts, and reproach the Creator for those which may be harmful to our life? And shall we not reflect that all has not been created in view of the wants of our bellies?

Hexaemeron 5.4

"And God made two great lights." To the sun the properties of the moon are near akin; she, too, has an immense body, whose splendor only yields to that of the sun. Our eyes, however, do not always see her in her full size. Now she presents a perfectly rounded disc, now when diminished and lessened she shows a deficiency on one side.

It is not without a secret reason of the divine Maker of the universe, that the moon appears from time to time under such different forms. It presents a striking example of our nature. Nothing is stable in man; here from nothingness he raises himself to perfection; there after having hasted to put forth his strength to attain his full greatness he suddenly is subject to gradual deterioration, and is destroyed by diminution. Thus, the sight of the moon, making us think of the rapid vicissitudes of human things, ought to teach us not to pride ourselves on the good things of this life.

Hexaemeron 6.10

"And God said, Let the waters bring forth abundantly the moving creature that hath life" after their kind, "and fowl that may fly above the earth" after their kind.

The command was given, and immediately the rivers and lakes becoming fruitful brought forth their natural broods; the sea travailed with all kinds of swimming creatures; not even in mud and marshes did the water remain idle; it took its part in creation. Everywhere from its ebullition frogs, gnats and flies came forth. For that which we see today is the sign of the past. Thus everywhere the water hastened to obey the Creator's command.

Hexaemeron 7.1

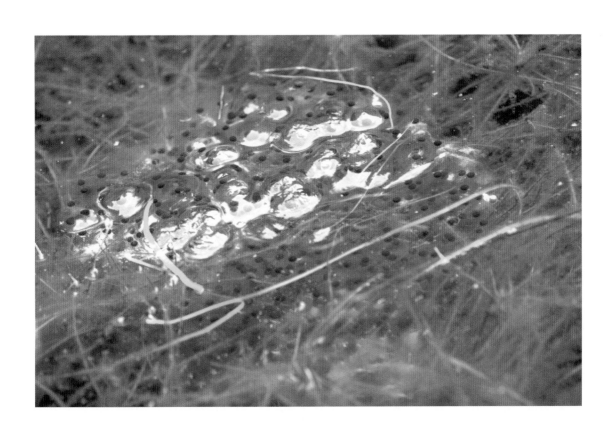

How is it that each sort of fish, content with the region that has been assigned to it, never travels over its own limits to pass into foreign seas? No surveyor has ever distributed to them their habitations, nor enclosed them in walls, nor assigned limits to them; each kind has been naturally assigned its own home. One gulf nourishes one kind of fish, another other sorts; those which swarm here are absent elsewhere. No mountain raises its sharp peaks between them; no rivers bar the passage to them; it is a law of nature, which according to the needs of each kind, has allotted to them their dwelling places with equality and justice.

It is not thus with us. Why? Because we incessantly move the ancient landmarks which our fathers have set. We encroach, we add house to house, field to field, to enrich ourselves at the expense of our neighbor.

Hexaemeron 7.3-4

Instances have, however, been known of migratory fish, who, as if common deliberation transported them into strange regions, all start on their march at a given sign. When the time marked for breeding arrives, they, as if awakened by a common law of nature, migrate from gulf to gulf, directing their course toward the North Sea… Who puts them in marching array? Where is the prince's order? Has an edict affixed in the public place indicated to them their day of departure? Who serves them as a guide? See how the divine order embraces all and extends to the smallest object. A fish does not resist God's law, and we men cannot endure His precepts of salvation! Do not despise fish because they are dumb and quite unreasoning; rather fear lest, in your resistance to the disposition of the Creator, you have even less reason than they. Listen to the fish, who by their actions all but speak and say: it is for the perpetuation of our race that we undertake this long voyage. They have not the gift of reason, but they have the law of nature firmly seated within them, to show them what they have to do.

Hexaemeron 7.4

And God said
"Let the earth bring forth the living creature
after his kind, cattle and creeping things, and
beast of the earth after his kind; and it was so."
The command of God advanced step by step
and earth thus received her adornment.

Take the bee for your model, which constructs
its cells without injuring anyone and without
interfering with the goods of others. It gathers
openly wax from the flowers with its mouth,
drawing in the honey scattered over them like
dew, and injects it into the hollow of its cells…
The book of Proverbs has given the bee the most
honorable and the best praise by calling
her wise and industrious.

After having spread the wax like a thin
membrane, she distributes it in contiguous
compartments which, weak though they are,
by their number and by their mass, sustain the
whole edifice… See how the discoveries of
geometry are mere by-works to the wise bee!

Hexaemeron 8.1, 8.4

*W*hat have you to say, you who do not believe in the change that Paul promises you in the resurrection, when you see so many metamorphoses among creatures of the air? What are we not told of the horned worm of India! First it changes into a caterpillar, then becomes a buzzing insect, and not content with this form, it clothes itself, instead of wings, with loose, broad plates… Remember the metamorphoses of this creature, conceive a clear idea of the resurrection, and do not refuse to believe in the change that Paul announces for all men.

Hexaemeron 8.8

he earth is the Lord's and the fulness thereof." O God, enlarge within us the sense of fellowship with all living things, our brothers the animals to whom Thou hast given the earth as their home in common with us. We remember with shame that in the past we have exercised the high dominion of man with ruthless cruelty, so that the voice of the earth, which should have gone up to Thee in song, has been a groan of travail. May we realize that they live, not for us alone, but for themselves and for Thee, and that they love the sweetness of life.

Liturgy of St. Basil

John Chrysostom

In John Chrysostom (354?-407) there was a happy blend of sterling character and golden-mouthed pulpit oratory. He was born in Antioch, attended excellent schools, and eventually set out on a promising legal career. But he was soon to follow the lead of Basil, his college companion, and at about age twenty he abandoned the pursuit of "vain verbosity" and became a monk. Chrysostom then left the city for the seclusion of the mountains south of Antioch. There he spent the next few years living a largely solitary life in the occasional company of other monks, including an old Syrian, Hesychius, whose name, meaning "stillness," signified the inner quality that Chrysostom sought. After he injured his health through some over-zealous asceticism, he returned to Antioch, became a priest, and preached brilliantly for years. Then, in 398, he was suddenly appointed archbishop of Constantinople. Because of his attempts in this capacity to reform the clergy, to support the needy, and to curb the immorality of the Roman court, he lost favor with both ecclesiastical and civil authorities and in 404 was banished and spent his last years in exile.

Words flowed from Chrysostom's pen as freely as from his lips, and his writings comprise the largest literary output of all the Eastern Fathers. The wonder of the earth enters into his works at various points. In his sermons entitled *On the Incomprehensible Nature of God*, he emphasizes that the immensity of the Creator, "who dwells in unapproachable light," surpasses even the magnitude and mystery of the creation. He presents a more detailed consideration of the material world in the series of sermons called *On the Statues*, which he delivered in the old Apostolic Church in Antioch in the spring of 387, during a period of great social upheaval that involved the toppling of the statues of the Emperor and his wife. Here he offers his audience guidance and hope, in part by directing their eyes to the world of nature seen in light of Paul's assertion in Romans 1:20 that "ever since the creation of the world His eternal power and divine nature, invisible though they are, have been understood and seen through the things He has made."

God not only produced the creation but He holds together what He produced. Whether you are speaking about the angels, archangels, the powers above, or simply every creature both visible and invisible, they all enjoy the benefit of His providence. And if they are ever deprived of that providential action, they waste away, they perish, they are gone.

The Incomprehensible Nature of God 12.51

*S*uppose the world to be a ship; the earth to be placed below as the keel; the sky to be the sail; men to be the passengers; the subjacent abyss, the sea. How is it then that during so long a time, no shipwreck has taken place? Now let a ship go one day without a pilot and crew, and thou will see it straightway foundering!

For if a ship does not hold together without a pilot, but soon founders, how could the world have held together so long a time if there was no one governing its course?

On the Statues 10.5

He has placed His creation in the midst, before the eyes of all men; in order that they may guess at the Creator from His works…This it was which the prophet signified when he said, "The heavens declare the glory of God." How then, tell me, do they declare it? Voice they have none; mouth they possess not; no tongue is theirs! How then do they declare? By means of the spectacle itself. For when thou sees the beauty, the breadth, the height, the position, the form, the stability thereof during so long a period; hearing as it were a voice, and being instructed by the spectacle, thou adores Him who created a body so fair and strange! The heavens may be silent, but the sight of them emits a voice that is louder than a trumpet's sound.

On the Statues 9.4

ontemplate with me the beauty of the sky; how it has been preserved so long without being dimmed; and remains as bright and clear as if it had been only fabricated today; moreover, the power of the earth, how its womb has not become effete by bringing forth during so long a time! Contemplate with me the fountains; how they burst forth and fail not, since the time they were begotten, to flow forth continually throughout the day and night! Contemplate with me the sea, receiving so many rivers, yet never exceeding its measure.

On the Statues 10.5

ollow me while I enumerate the meadows, the gardens, the various tribes of flowers; all sorts of herbs, and their uses; their odors, forms, disposition, yea, but their very names; the trees which are fruitful, and which are barren; the nature of metals,—and of animals,— in the sea, or on the land; of those that swim, and those that traverse the air; the mountains, the forests, the groves; the meadow below, and the meadow above; for there is a meadow on the earth, and a meadow too in the sky; the various flowers of the stars; the rose below, and the rainbow above!

On the Statues 10.5

*W*ho can describe the perfect order of the seasons; and how these … succeed one another with the happiest harmony; and how those who are in the middle cease not to pass over to the opposite ones with a gradual and noiseless transition? … For since sudden changes to opposite extremes are productive of the worst injury and disease, God has contrived that after winter we should take up the spring, and after the spring the summer; and after the summer the autumn; and thus transport us to winter, so that these changes from seasons which are opposite, should come upon us harmlessly and by degrees, through the aid of intermediate ones.

On the Statues 9.6

97

avid said of the sun, that "he is as a bridegroom coming out of his chamber, and rejoiceth as a giant to run his course." See thou how he places before thee the beauty of this star, and its greatness? For even as a bridegroom when he appears from some stately chamber, so the sun sends forth his rays under the East; and adorning the heaven as it were with a saffron-colored veil, and making the clouds like roses, and running unimpeded all the day; he meets no obstacle to interrupt his course. Behold thou, then, his beauty? Behold thou his greatness? Look also at the proof of his weakness! ... Often, at least, when a cloud passes underneath him, though emitting his beams, and endeavoring to pierce through it, he has not strength to do so; the cloud being too dense, and not suffering him to penetrate through it.

Thou see how God has provided for us on either hand; leading us by the beauty of the elements to the knowledge of His divinity; and, by their feebleness, not permitting us to lapse into worship of them.

On the Statues 10.8, 10.10

The nature of the clouds is one, but the things which are produced out of them are different. For the rain, indeed, becomes wine in the grape, but oil in the olive. And in other plants is changed into their juices; and the womb of the earth is one, and yet bears different fruits. The heat, too, of the sunbeams is one, but it ripens all things differently; bringing some to maturity more slowly, and others more quickly. Who then but must feel astonishment and admiration at these things?

On the Statues 12.4

What I affirmed respecting the creation, I affirm also respecting the body, that both these things alike excite my admiration of God; that He has made it corruptible; and that in its very corruptibility, He has manifested His own power and wisdom… since He has introduced such a harmony of parts in clay and ashes, and senses so various and manifold and capable of such spiritual wisdom.

The Supreme Artist, from the same material of which only the brick and tile is formed, has been able to make an eye so beautiful, as to astonish all who behold it, and to implant in it such power, that it can at once survey the high aerial expanse, and by the aid of a small pupil embrace the mountains, forests, hills, the ocean, yea, the heaven, by so small a thing!

On the Statues 11.5-6

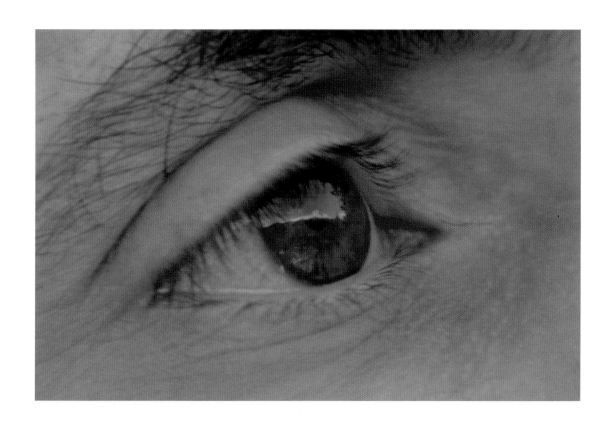

It wasn't simply for our use that He produced all things; instead, it was also for our benefit in the sense that we might see the overflowing abundance of His creatures and be overwhelmed at the Creator's power, and be in a position to know that all these things were produced by a certain wisdom and ineffable love...

In the case of the seeds and the plants, the earth has produced not only fruitbearing trees but also those giving no fruit, and brings forth not only crops that are profitless but also some that are strange to us and ones that are in many cases harmful. But no one will presume to find fault with their creation on that account; after all, they have not been produced without rhyme or reason. I mean, they would not have received commendation from the Lord had they not been created to serve some need.

...there is nothing that has been created without some reason, even if human nature is incapable of knowing precisely the reason for them all.

Homilies on Genesis 7.13, 7.14

From the creation learn to admire thy Lord! And if any of the things thou see exceed thy comprehension, and thou are not able to find the reason thereof, yet for this glorify the Creator, that the wisdom of these works surpasses thine understanding.

On the Statues 12.7

Augustine

The life of Augustine (354-430) is one of the most well-known and influential lives in the history of Christianity, due in large part to his autobiographical *Confessions.* There he relates the searching inner story of his soul from his birth at Tagaste in North Africa, where his mother, Monica, raised him as a Christian, his profligate days as a student of rhetoric in Carthage during which he abandoned his religion, his growing passion for philosophy and his embracing of the Manichean system, his years of teaching and intellectual ferment in Rome and Milan, to his eventual return to the faith and his baptism on Easter Eve in 387. He spent the remainder of his life in Hippo, near Tagaste, serving as priest and bishop, and writing voluminously, works that have established him as the foremost Western Church Father and, in the eyes of many, second only to Saint Paul with regard to his influence on Christianity.

In Augustine's other best-known book, *The City of God*, he presents his vast Christian vision of history as the spiritual movement from the "City of Man" to the "City of God," from the restlessness of self love to the restfulness of divine love. For Augustine, however, especially in his mature thought, the story of human redemption takes place within the larger history of the whole creation. Rejecting the Manichean separation of reality into a spiritual good and a material evil, Augustine, in a manner reminiscent of Irenaeus, emphasized the immanent creativity of God in both the origin and sustenance of the earth, and looked forward to the emergence of a new creation. Though the cosmic Word and Spirit are eternally at work throughout the material order, the citizens of the City of God will see with new eyes—and will smell, taste, touch, and hear with new bodies—the fullness of the divine presence and providence in the patterns of the natural world.

God, Thou made heaven and earth in Thy Word, in Thy Son, in Thy Power, in Thy Wisdom, in Thy Truth—speaking in a wondrous way and making in a wondrous way. Who will understand it? Who will give an account of it? What is that Light which shines intermittently within me and pierces my heart without any wound? I am moved to feel both terror and ardor: I feel terror in so far as I am unlike it, ardor in so far as I am like it. Wisdom, it is Wisdom Itself which comes at times to enlighten me, cutting through my beclouded darkness...

Confessions 11.9

What beauty for contemplation and what bounties for use God has scattered like largesse for man amid the weariness and miseries of his fallen and penalized lot! What words can describe the myriad beauties of land and sea and sky? Just think of the illimitable abundance and the marvelous loveliness of light, or of the beauty of the sun and moon and stars, of shadowy glades in the woods and of the colors and perfume of flowers, of the songs and plumage of so many varieties of birds, of the innumerable animals of every species that amaze us most when they are smallest in size. For example, the activity of ants and bees seems more stupendous than the sheer immensity of whales. Or take a look at the grandiose spectacle of the open sea, clothing and reclothing itself in dresses of changing shades of green and purple and blue.

The City of God 22.24

*H*is sovereignty and power reach to the lowest things. All things that grow and sustain animal life, both liquids and solids, He produced and made appropriate for different natures. He gave us the earth, the fertility of soil, and foods for men and beasts. All causes, primary and secondary, come within His knowledge and control.

The City of God 7.30

Even when tiny bacteria spring from the corpse of a larger animal, it is by the same law of the Creator that all these minute bodies serve in peace the organic wholes of which they are parts. Even when the flesh of dead animals is eaten by other animals, there is no change in the universal laws which are meant for the common good of every kind of life, the common good that is effected by bringing like into peace with like. It makes no difference what disintegrating forces are at work, or what new combinations are made, or even what changes or transformations are effected.

The City of God 19.12

The truth is that all these actions and energies belong to the one true God, who is really a God, who is wholly present everywhere, is confined by no frontiers and bound by no hindrances, is indivisible and immutable, and, though Hisnature has no need of either heaven or of earth, He fills them both with His presence and His power.

The City of God 7.30

The explanation, then, of the goodness of creation is the goodness of God. It is a reasonable and sufficient explanation whether considered in the light of philosophy or of faith. It puts an end to all controversies concerning the origin of the world. Nevertheless, certain heretics remain unconvinced, on the ground that many things in creation are unsuitable and even harmful to that poor and fragile mortality of the flesh which, of course, is no more than the just penalty of sin. The heretics mention, for example, fire, cold, wild beasts, and things like that, without considering how wonderful such things are in themselves and in their proper place and how beautifully they fit into the total pattern of the universe, making, as it were, their particular contributions to the commonweal of cosmic beauty.

The City of God 11.22

s there anything, in fact, more beautiful than a leaping, luminous flame of fire? Or anything more useful, when it warms us, heals us, cooks our food? Yet, nothing is more painful when it burns us. Thus, the same thing applied in one way is harmful, but when properly used is extremely beneficial. It is all but impossible to enumerate all the good uses to which fire is put throughout the world.

We should pay no attention to those who praise fire for its light but condemn its heat—on the principle that a thing should be judged not by its nature, but by our comfort or inconvenience. They like to see it, but hate to be burnt. What they forget is that the same light which they like is injurious and unsuitable for weak eyes, and that the heat which they hate is, for some animals, the proper condition for a healthy life.

The City of God 12.4

*W*e see that the face of the earth is adorned by earthly animals, and that man, in Thy image and likeness, is placed above all irrational living things by this image and likeness of Thine, namely, the power of reason and understanding.

Confessions 13.32

Thus man is "renewed unto the knowledge of God, according to the image of his Creator," and becoming "the spiritual man judges all things" (those which are to be judged, of course)... Now, that he "judges all things,"—that means that he has dominion over the fish of the sea and the fowl that fly in the heavens, and all domestic and wild animals, and every part of the earth, and all creeping creatures that move upon the earth. This he exercises by virtue of the understanding of his mind, through which he "perceives the things that are of the Spirit of God."

Confessions 13.22-23

In the city of the world both the rulers themselves and the people they dominate are dominated by the lust for domination; whereas in the City of God all citizens serve one another in charity... Hence, even the wise men in the city of man live according to man, and their only goal has been the goods of their bodies or of the mind or of both... In the City of God, on the contrary, there is no merely human wisdom, but there is a piety which worships the true God as He should be worshiped and has as its goal that reward of all holiness whether in the society of saints on earth or in that of angels of heaven, which is "that God may be all in all."

The City of God 14.28

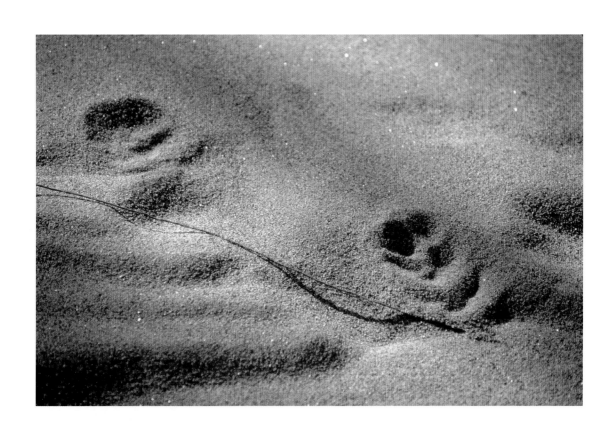

"He was in the world, and the world was made through Him." Do not imagine that He was in the world in such a way as the earth is in the world, the sky is in the world, the sun, the moon, and the stars are in the world, trees, cattle, and men are in the world. He was not in the world in such a way. But how was He? As the master builder who governs what He has made. For He did not make it in the way a craftsman makes a chest. The chest which he makes is external to him; and when it is constructed, it has been situated in another place. And however nearby he is, he who is constructing it sits in another place and is external to that which he is constructing.

But God constructs while infused in the world. He constructs while situated everywhere. He does not withdraw from anywhere; He does not direct the structure which He constructs as someone on the outside. By the presence of His majesty He makes what He makes; by His own presence He governs what He has made.

Tractates on the Gospel of John 2.10

Certain seeds of all the things which are generated in a corporeal and visible fashion lie hidden in the corporeal elements of this world... The Creator of the invisible seeds is the Creator of all things Himself; since whatever things become visible to our eyes by being born receive the first beginning of their course from hidden seeds, and take their gradual growth to their proper size and their own distinctive forms, according to the rules that have been fixed as it were from the beginning.

The Trinity 3.8

For as mothers are pregnant with unborn offspring, so the world itself is pregnant with the causes of unborn beings, which are not created in it except from that highest essence, where nothing is either born or dies, begins to be or ceases to be.

The Trinity 3.9

*L*et us, then, consider the beauty of any tree in its trunk, branches, leaves, and fruit. This tree surely did not spring forth suddenly in this size and form, but rather went through a process of growth with which we are familiar. For it sprouted forth from a root which a germ or bud first planted in the earth, and from that source the tree took its shape as it developed with all its parts. Furthermore, the germ was from a seed, and therefore in the seed all those parts existed primordially, not in the dimensions of bodily mass but as a force and causal power.

In the seed, then, there was invisibly present all that would develop in time into a tree. And in this same way we must picture the world, when God made all things together, as having had all things together which were made in it and with it when day was made. This includes not only heaven with sun, moon, and stars, whose splendor remains unchanged as they move in a circular motion; and earth and the deep waters, which are in almost unceasing motion, and which, placed below the sky, make up the lower part of the world; but it includes also the beings which water and earth produced in potency and in their causes before they came forth in the course of time as they have become known to us in the works which God even now produces.

The Literal Meaning of Genesis 5.23

The miracle of our Lord, Jesus Christ, by which He made wine from water is certainly no wonder for those who know that God did it. For He, the very one who every year does this on vines, made wine on that day at the wedding in those six water jars, which He ordered to be filled with water. For just as what the attendants put into the water jars was turned into wine by the Lord's effort so also what the clouds pour down is turned into wine by the effort of the same Lord. But that does not amaze us because it happens every year; by its regularity it has lost its wonderment. Yet it merits even greater reflection than that which was done in the water jars.

For who is there who reflects upon the works of God, by which this whole world is governed and managed, and is not struck dumb and overwhelmed by miracles?

Tractates on the Gospel of John 8.1

God does not work under the limits of time by motions of body and soul, as do men and angels, but by the eternal, unchangeable, and fixed exemplars of His coeternal Word and by a kind of brooding action of His equally coeternal Holy Spirit. The Greek and Latin translations say of the Holy Spirit that "He was stirring above the waters;" but in Syriac, which is close to Hebrew, …the rendering is not "He was stirring above" but rather "He was brooding over." This action is not like that of a person who nurses swellings or wounds with the proper application of cold or hot water; but it is rather like that of a bird that broods over its eggs, the mother somehow helping in the development of her young by the warmth from her body, through an affection similar to that of love.

The Literal Meaning of Genesis 1.18

y mouth shall speak the praise of the Lord, of that Lord by whom all things were made and who was made flesh amid all the works of His hands; …The Word as God existing before all time, the Word as flesh existing only for an allotted time; the Creator of the sun created under the light of the sun; …Maker of heaven and earth brought forth on this earth overshadowed by the heavens; unspeakably wise, wisely speechless; filling the whole world, lying in a manger; guiding the stars, a nursling at the breast; though insignificant in the form of man, so great in the form of God that his greatness was not lessened by His insignificance nor was His smallness crushed by His might. When He assumed human form He did not abandon His divine operations, nor did He cease to reach "from end to end mightily and to order all things sweetly." When clothed in the weakness of our flesh He was received, not imprisoned, in the Virgin's womb so that without the Food of Wisdom being withdrawn from the angels we might taste how sweet is the Lord.

Sermons on the Liturgical Seasons—"A Christmas Sermon" 187

John of Damascus

With John of Damascus (679?-749) the great era of the Church Fathers came to a close. Born amid the splendor of the Court in Damascus, John inherited the high office his father had held and for a period carried out the duties of his powerful position with interest and ease. But his heart was not content, partly because a Sicilian monk named Cosmas, who had been his childhood tutor, had instilled in him a sense of deeper treasures. Finally, around the year 726, he sold his many possessions, gave the money to the poor, and entered the monastery of Saint Sava, high up in the desert hills of Palestine. He happily remained there for the rest of his life, writing a flood of homilies, commentaries, theological tracts, and hymns in a Greek so elegant that he earned the epithet Chrysorrhoas, "gold-pouring." He is recognized as a saint by both the Eastern and Western Churches and he formed an important link between Greek antiquity and the Latin Middle Ages.

John's sense of the sacralizing effect of the divine presence in the material world is at the root of his spiritual life and written work. He devoted much ink to a spirited defense of the Orthodox veneration of icons, countering the forces of iconoclasm by proclaiming that "I do not worship matter; I worship the Creator of matter who became matter for my sake, who willed to take his abode in matter; who worked out my salvation through matter. Never will I cease honoring the matter which wrought my salvation! ...Do not despise matter, for it is not despicable. God has made nothing despicable."* In his most famous work, the *Exposition of the Orthodox Faith*, he lays out his comprehensive vision of a Christian cosmology. He integrates into his description of the natural world the widespread ancient doctrine of the four elements—earth, water, air, fire— elements which perhaps spoke with a bare eloquence at Saint Sava, where the dry desert dust turned to mud with the winter rains and the scorching summer heat baked the airy cliffs of the Valley of Fire. For John, the modulating harmony of these opposing elements in the structure of all things was resounding evidence of the divine pulse at the heart of matter.

*St. John of Damascus, *On the Divine Images*, trans. by David Anderson (Crestwood, N.Y.: St. Vladimir's Seminary Press, 1980), 23, 24.

Our God Himself,
whom we glorify as Three in One, "created the
heaven and the earth and all that they contain,"
and brought all things out of nothing into being:
some He made out of no pre-existing basis of
matter, such as heaven, earth, air, fire, water:
and the rest out of these elements that He had
created, such as living creatures, plants, seeds.
For these are made up of earth, and water,
and air, and fire, at the bidding of the Creator.

The Orthodox Faith 2.5

Fire is one of the four elements, light and with a greater tendency to ascend than the others. It has the power of burning and also of giving light, and it was made by the Creator on the first day... In the beginning, then, ...God created light, the ornament and glory of the whole visible creation. For take away light and all things remain in undistinguishable darkness, incapable of displaying their native beauty.

The Orthodox Faith 2.7

*A*ir is the most subtle element, and is moist and warm; heavier, indeed, than fire, but lighter than earth and water. It is the cause of respiration and voice: it is colorless, that is, it has no color by nature: it is clear and transparent, for it is capable of receiving light... and its movements in space are up, down, within, without, to the right and to the left, and the cyclical movement. ...And wind is a movement of air: or wind is a rush of air which changes its name as it changes the place whence it rushes.

The Orthodox Faith 2.8

ater is also one of
the four elements, the most beautiful of God's
creations. It is both wet and cold, heavy, and
with a tendency to descend, and flows with great
readiness. It is this the Holy Scripture has in
view when it says, "And darkness was upon the
face of the deep. And the Spirit of God moved
upon the face of the waters."

Water, then, is the most beautiful element and
rich in usefulness, and purifies from all filth, and
not only from the filth of the body but from that
of the soul, if it should have received the grace of
the Spirit.

The Orthodox Faith 2.9

The birds form a link between water and earth and air: for they have their origin in the water, they live on the earth and they fly in the air.

The Orthodox Faith 2.9

The earth is one of the four elements, dry, cold, heavy, motionless, brought into being by God, out of nothing on the first day.

Some hold that the earth is in the form of a sphere, others that it is in that of a cone. At all events it is much smaller than the heaven, and suspended almost like a point in its midst. And it will pass away and be changed. But blessed is the man who inherits the earth promised to the meek.

For the earth that is to be the possession of the holy is immortal. Who, then, can fitly marvel at the boundless and incomprehensible wisdom of the Creator? Or who can render sufficient thanks to the Giver of so many blessings?

The Orthodox Faith 2.10

He creates with His own hands man of a visible nature and an invisible, after His own image and likeness: on the one hand man's body He formed of earth, and on the other his reasoning and thinking soul He bestowed upon him by His own inbreathing, and this is what we mean by "after His image."

Man, it is to be noted, has community with things inanimate, and participates in the life of unreasoning creatures, and shares in the mental processes of those endowed with reason. For the bond of union between man and inanimate things is the body and its composition out of the four elements. And the bond between man and plants consists, in addition to these things, of their powers of nourishment and growth and seeding, that is, generation. And finally, over and above these links, man is connected with unreasoning animals by appetite, that is anger and desire, and sense and impulsive movement.

Lastly, man's reason unites him to incorporeal and intelligent natures, for he applies his reason and mind and judgement to everything, and pursues after virtues, and eagerly follows after piety, which is the crown of the virtues. And so man is a microcosm.

God, then, made man without evil, upright, virtuous, free from pain and care, glorified with every virtue, adorned with all that is good, like a sort of second microcosm within the great world, another angel capable of worship, compound, surveying the visible creation and initiated into the mysteries of the realm of thought, king over the things of earth, but subject to a higher king, of the earth and of the heaven.

*L*ife itself, is should be observed, is energy, yea, the primal energy of the living creature; and so is the whole economy of the living creature, its functions of nutrition and growth, that is, the vegetative side of its nature, and the movement stirred by impulse, that is, the sentient side, and its activity of intellect and free will. Energy, moreover, is the perfect realization of power.

And so in connection with our Lord Jesus Christ, the power of miracles is the energy of His divinity, while the work of His hands and the willing and the saying ...are the energy of His humanity. And if the providence that embraces all creation is not only of the Father and the Holy Spirit, but also of the Son even after the incarnation, assuredly since that is energy, He must have even after the incarnation the same energy as the Father.

The Orthodox Faith 3.15

The very continuity of the creation, and its preservation and government, teach us that there does exist a Deity, who supports and maintains and preserves and ever provides for this universe. For how could opposite natures, such as fire and water, air and earth, have combined with each other so as to form one complete world, and continue to abide in indissoluble union, were there not some omnipotent power which bound them together and always is preserving them from dissolution?

The Orthodox Faith 1.3

God, who is good and altogether good and more than good, who is goodness throughout, by reason of the exceeding riches of His goodness did not suffer Himself, that is His nature, only to be good, with no other to participate therein, but because of this He made first the spiritual and heavenly powers; next the visible and sensible universe; next man with his spiritual and sentient nature. All things, therefore, which He made, share in His goodness in respect of their existence. For He Himself is existence to all, since all things that are, are in Him, not only because it was He that brought them out of nothing into being, but because His energy preserves and maintains all that He made.

The Orthodox Faith 4.13

Resources

Books

The following books are a sampling of the many that deal, from varied and sometimes conflicting viewpoints, with the ecological implications of Christianity. This list contains a number of important general works, along with studies that focus more specifically on the ancient world, particularly on issues of biblical interpretation and the ideas of the Church Fathers.

Berry, Thomas. *The Dream of the Earth.* San Francisco: Sierra Club, 1988.

Berry, Thomas, with Thomas Clarke. *Befriending the Earth: A Theology of Reconciliation Between Humans and the Earth.* Mystic, Conn.: Twenty-Third Publications, 1991.

Berry, Wendell. *A Continuous Harmony: Essays Cultural and Agricultural.* New York: Harcourt Brace Jovanovich, 1970, 1972.

_____.*The Gift of Good Land: Further Essays Cultural and Agricultural.* San Francisco: North Point, 1981.

Brueggeman, Walter. *The Land: Place as Gift, Promise, and Challenge in Biblical Faith.* Philadelphia: Fortress, 1977.

Cobb, John B., Jr. *Sustaining the Common Good: A Christian Perspective on the Global Economy.* Cleveland, Ohio: Pilgrim, 1994.

DeWitt, Calvin B., ed. *The Environment and the Christian: What Can We Learn from the New Testament?* Grand Rapids, Mich.: Baker Book House, 1991.

Fox, Matthew. *The Coming of the Cosmic Christ.* San Francisco: HarperSanFrancisco, 1988.

_____.*Creation Spirituality: Liberating Gifts for the Peoples of the Earth.* San Francisco: HarperSanFrancisco, 1991.

Gilkey, Langdon. *Maker of Heaven and Earth: A Study of the Christian Doctrine of Creation.* Garden City, N.Y.: Doubleday, 1959.

Gregorios, Paulos. *The Human Presence: An Orthodox View of Nature.* Geneva: World Council of Churches, 1978.

LaChance, Albert J., and John E. Carroll, eds. *Embracing Earth: Catholic Approaches to Ecology.* Maryknoll, N.Y.: Orbis, 1994.

McFague, Sallie. *The Body of God: An Ecological Theology.* Minneapolis: Fortress, 1993.

Moltmann, Jurgen. *God in Creation: A New Theology of Creation and the Spirit of God.* San Francisco: Harper and Row, 1985.

Nash, James A. *Loving Nature: Ecological Integrity and Christian Responsibility.* Nashville: Abingdon, 1991.

Perdue, Leo G. *Wisdom and Creation: The Theology of Wisdom Literature.* Nashville: Abingdon, 1994.

Regenstein, Lewis G. *Replenish the Earth: A History of Organized Religion's Treatment of Animals and Nature—Including the Bible's Message of Conservation and Kindness Toward Animals.* New York: Crossroad, 1991.

Reuther, Rosemary Radford. *Gaia and God: An Ecofeminist Theology of Earth Healing.* New York: HarperCollins, 1992.

Rockefeller, Steven C, and John C. Elder, eds. *Spirit and Nature: Why the Environment is a Religious Issue—An Interfaith Dialogue.* Boston: Beacon Press, 1992.

Santmire, H. Paul. *Brother Earth: Nature, God, and Ecology in a Time of Crisis.* New York: Thomas Nelson, 1970.

_____. *The Travail of Nature: The Ambiguous Ecological Promise of Christian Theology.* Minneapolis: Fortress, 1985.

Sherrard, Philip. *The Eclipse of Man and Nature.* Ipswich: Golgonooza Press, 1987.

_____. *Human Image/World Image: The Death and Resurrection of Sacred Cosmology.* Ipswich: Golgonooza Press, 1993.

Sittler, Joseph. *Essays on Nature and Grace.* Philadelphia: Fortress, 1972.

Swimme, Brian, and Thomas Berry. *The Universe Story: From the Primordial Flaring Forth to the Ecozoic Era.* New York: HarperCollins, 1992.

Wilkinson, Loren, ed. *Earthkeeping in the '90s: Stewardship of Creation.* Grand Rapids, Mich.: Eerdmans, 1991.

Epiphany Journal often contains articles that analyze and promote an ecological Christianity, particularly from an Eastern Orthodox perspective. Three issues have been devoted wholly to this topic: Vol. 6, no. 1 (Fall 1985); Vol. 8, no. 2 (Winter 1988); Vol. 10, no. 3 (Spring 1990). They can be ordered from Epiphany Press, P.O. Box 2250, South Portland, ME 04116-2250, (207) 767-1889.

Organizations

The burgeoning interest in the connection between religion and environmentalism in recent years has blossomed into numerous local, regional, national, and international groups and organizations, many of which publish newsletters or magazines. The following are some of the leading interdenominational organizations. Those that accept individual memberships are marked with an asterisk (*).

* Center for Respect of Life and Environment
2100 L. Street, NW
Washington, DC 20037
(202) 778-6133
(An affiliate of the Humane Society of the United States)

* Christian Environmental Association
1650 Zanker Road,
Suite 150
San Jose, CA 95112
(408) 441-1571

* Christian Society of the Green Cross
10 East Lancaster Avenue
Wynnewood, PA 19096
(610) 645-9390

Eco-Justice Working Group
National Council of Churches
475 Riverside Drive
New York, NY 10115
(212) 870-2141

* Evangelical Environmental Network
10 East Lancaster Avenue
Wynnewood, PA 19096
(610) 645-9393

* **Friends of Creation Spirituality**
  Box 19216
  Oakland, CA 94619
  (510) 482-4984

* **Interfaith Council for the Protection of Animals and Nature**
  4290 Raintree Lane, NW
  Atlanta, GA 30327
  (404) 252-9176

* **International Network for Religion and Animals**
  c/o Dr. Marc A. Wessels
  P.O. Box 1335
  North Wales, PA 19454
  (215) 721-1908

National Religious Partnership for the Environment
1047 Amsterdam Avenue
New York, NY 10025
(212) 316-7441
The N.R.P.E. is comprised of four member groups:
- The U.S. Catholic Conference
- The National Council of the Churches of Christ in the USA
- The Coalition on the Environment and Jewish Life
- The Evangelical Environmental Network
It publishes a very useful *Directory of Environmental Activities and Resources in the North American Religious Community.*

* **North American Coalition on Religion and Ecology**
  5 Thomas Circle, NW
  Washington, DC 20005
  (202) 462-2591

* **North American Conference on Christianity and Ecology**
  P.O. Box 40011
  St. Paul, MN 55104
  (612) 698-0349

Educational Opportunities

The study centers listed below offer a variety of programs to broaden and deepen awareness of the ties between ecological and spiritual concerns.

Au Sable Institute
7526 Sunset Trail NE
Mancelona, MI 49659
(608) 255-0950

Centre for Ecology and Spirituality at Holy Cross
R.R. 1
Port Burwell, Ontario N0J 1TO
(519) 874-4502

Gaia Institute
Cathedral of St. John the Divine
1047 Amsterdam Ave. at 112th St.
New York, NY 10025
(212) 295-1930

Sophia Center
Holy Names College
Oakland, CA 94619
(510) 436-1046

Schumacher College
The Old Postern, Dartington
Totnes
Devon TQ9 6EA
UK
Tel. 0803-865934

Seattle University
Ecological Studies Program
Broadway and Madison
Seattle, WA 98122

Notes on the Photographs

The photographs were made with Pentax 35mm equipment using a combination of lenses ranging from 24mm to 420mm, often with a polarizing filter. I use Fujichrome Velvia film almost exclusively.

Credits

The text selections in this book have been drawn from the following sources. Grateful acknowledgement is made to publishers as indicated for permission to reprint copyrighted material.

All the Scripture quotations in Pa\ from the New Revised Standard Version of the Bible, copyright © 1989, by the Division of Christian Education of the National Council of the Churches of Christ in the U.S.A., and used by permission. All rights reserved.

St. Irenaeus, *Against Heresies and Fragments from the Lost Writings*. Translated by Alexander Roberts and James Donaldson. In *The Ante-Nicene Fathers*, Vol. 1. Copyright © 1885. Reprint. Grand Rapids, Mich.: Wm. B. Eerdmans, 1979.

St. Basil, *The Hexaemeron*. Translated by Blomfield Jackson. In *A Select Library of Nicene and Post-Nicene Fathers*, 2d ser., Vol. 8. Copyright © 1895. Reprint. Grand Rapids, Mich.: Wm. B. Eerdmans, 1978.

Liturgy of St. Basil. From the *UFAW Theological Bulletin* 2 (April 1962): 3.

St. John Chrysostom, *Homilies on Genesis*. Translated by Robert C. Hill. In *The Fathers of the Church*, Vol. 74. Copyright © 1986. Washington, D.C.: Catholic University of America Press. Reprinted by permission of the publisher.

St. John Chrysostom, *On the Incomprehensible Nature of God*. Translated by Paul W. Harkins. In *The Fathers of the Church*, Vol. 72. Copyright © 1984. Washington, D.C.: Catholic University of America Press. Reprinted by permission of the publisher.

St. John Chrysostom, *On the Statues*. Translated by W. R. W. Stephens. In *A Select Library of the Nicene and Post-Nicene Fathers*, 1st ser., Vol. 9. Copyright © 1889. Reprint. Grand Rapids, Mich.: Wm. B. Eerdmans, 1978.

St. Augustine, *The City of God*. Translated by Gerald G. Walsh et al. In *The Fathers of the Church*, Vols. 8, 14, 24. Copyright © 1950-54. Washington, D.C.: Catholic University of America Press. Reprinted by permission of the publisher.

St. Augustine, *Confessions*. Translated by Vernon J. Bourke. In *The Fathers of the Church*, Vol. 21. Copyright © 1953. Washington, D.C.: Catholic University of America Press. Reprinted by permission of the publisher.

St. Augustine, *The Literal Meaning of Genesis*. Translated by John Hammond Taylor. In *Ancient Christian Writers*, No. 41. Copyright © 1982. Mahwah, N.J.: Paulist Press. Reprinted by permission of the publisher.

St. Augustine, *Sermons on the Liturgical Seasons*. Translated by Mary Sarah Muldowney. In *The Fathers of the Church*, Vol. 38. Copyright © 1959. Washington, D.C.: Catholic University of America Press. Reprinted by permission of the publisher.

St. Augustine, *The Trinity*. Translated by Stephen McKenna. In *The Fathers of the Church*, Vol. 45. Copyright © 1963. Washington, D.C.: Catholic University of America Press. Reprinted by permission of the publisher.

St. Augustine, *Tractates on the Gospel of John*. Translated by John W. Rettig. In *The Fathers of the Church*, Vol. 78. Copyright © 1988. Washington, D.C.: Catholic University of America Press. Reprinted by permission of the publisher.

John of Damascus, *Exposition of the Orthodox Faith*. Translated by S. D. F. Salmond. In *A Select Library of Nicene and Post-Nicene Fathers*, 2d ser., Vol. 9. Copyright © 1899. Reprint. Grand Rapids, Mich.: Wm. B. Eerdmans, 1979.

John of Damascus, *On the Divine Images*. Translated by David Anderson. Copyright © 1980. Crestwood, N.Y.: St. Vladimir's Seminary Press. Reprinted by permission of the publisher.